THE CROSSING GUARD

IN FULL LIGHT

THE CROSSING GUARD

IN FULL LIGHT

BY DANIEL KARASIK

PLAYWRIGHTS CANADA PRESS
TORONTO

PLAYWRIGHTS CANADA PRESS
The Canadian Drama Publisher
215 Spadina Ave., Suite 230, Toronto, ON, Canada M5T 2C7
phone 416.703.0013 fax 416.408.3402
info@playwrightscanada.com • www.playwrightscanada.com

Playwrights Canada Press acknowledges the financial support of the Government of Canada through the Canada Book Fund and the Canada Council for the Arts, and of the Province of Ontario through the Ontario Arts Council and the Ontario Media Development Corporation, for our publishing activities.

 Canada Council   Conseil des Arts   ONTARIO ARTS COUNCIL
for the Arts   du Canada   CONSEIL DES ARTS DE L'ONTARIO

Canadä   Ontario
                  Ontario Media Development
                  Corporation

Cover design by Leah Renihan
Type design by Blake Sproule

LIBRARY AND ARCHIVES CANADA CATALOGUING IN PUBLICATION
Karasik, Daniel
The crossing guard ; &, In full light / Daniel Karasik.

Plays.
Issued also in electronic formats.
ISBN 978-1-77091-003-4

I. Title. II. Title: In full light.

PS8621.A6224C76 2011   C812'.6   C2011-905110-9

First edition: September 2011
Printed and bound in Canada by AGMV Marquis, Montreal

For my family.

THE
CROSSING
GUARD

The Crossing Guard was first presented by Tango Co. and Peanut Butter People on October 7, 2009, at the Tarragon Theatre Studio, Toronto, with the following cast and crew:

Timothy: Daniel Karasik
Jim: Gary Reineke
Miriam: Monica Dottor

Director: Anthony Furey
Lighting: André du Toit
Sound and music: Thomas Ryder Payne
Stage manager: Brooke Banning

The Crossing Guard was developed in part through the Canadian Stage Play Development Program with dramaturg Iris Turcott.

Characters (in order of appearance)

Timothy, seventeen
Jim, the crossing guard, retired
Miriam, mid-twenties

Note

An ellipsis (…) appearing on its own or before a line of dialogue indicates a silent, momentary response to what has just been said or not said.

Monday.

TIMOTHY and JIM, the crossing guard, stand at the crosswalk in front of the elementary school.

The light changes. JIM holds up his stop sign. He crosses the street and TIMOTHY crosses with him.

TIMOTHY   How's life?

JIM   Can't complain.

TIMOTHY   You probably could.

JIM   Why bother.

TIMOTHY   Pigeons still?

JIM   Pigeons, always.

TIMOTHY   How's Myrna?

JIM   Almost won the lottery.

TIMOTHY   Did she?

JIM   She had a couple numbers. Your cold better?

TIMOTHY   Oh, much.

                 He blows his nose violently.

                 Just because you mentioned it.

JIM   Sure.

TIMOTHY   They last, my colds.

JIM   I remember when you had one for the better part of a
                 year. When was that?

TIMOTHY   Five years ago.

JIM   You were twelve, thirteen.

TIMOTHY   Something like that.

JIM   It just lasted and lasted.

TIMOTHY   Winter was bad.

JIM   You should've stayed in.

TIMOTHY   Come on.

JIM   You should've given it a rest.

TIMOTHY   Look, your job.

                 *He points to the light. It's changed. JIM starts to go,
                 then stops when he sees TIMOTHY isn't following.*

JIM   What on earth?

TIMOTHY   I think maybe I'll just stick on this side this time.

JIM   You'll what?

TIMOTHY   I get tired of the back and forth.

JIM   Since when.

TIMOTHY   Since you started giving me advice.

JIM   Oh now really.

TIMOTHY   Go, your job, your job.

JIM   There's nobody here.

TIMOTHY   I'm here.

JIM   But you're not crossing.

TIMOTHY   You have a point.

JIM   Sure I do.

TIMOTHY   But then why did we cross the last time?

JIM   Because you wanted to.

TIMOTHY   No I didn't, I was following you.

JIM   Then why did I cross?

TIMOTHY   You were doing your job.

JIM   But there was nobody here!

TIMOTHY ...

JIM There was nobody here!

TIMOTHY ...

JIM I get tired. You know. I get tired.

TIMOTHY I was here.

JIM So you were.

A moment. TIMOTHY points to the light.

TIMOTHY Cross?

JIM Sure.

He holds up his sign. They cross.

TIMOTHY I found an analogue. You know: a parallel. Another one. This dog in Japan who'd meet his master every evening at Tokyo's Shibuya Station. Hachiko the dog. One day the master died. But Hachiko didn't know that. Every day he went back to the station. Every day he went and he waited for his master to arrive. For ten years. Ten years. He did that till he died.

JIM Well? Keep it up. You'll get there.

The light changes. JIM points.

It's up to you. Cross?

TIMOTHY Nah, I've had enough for today.

JIM   What a relief.

TIMOTHY   You have the time?

JIM   Always do. Quarter past four.

TIMOTHY   Good enough.

JIM   Not going to wait till the thirty?

TIMOTHY   Not today.

JIM   Suit yourself.

TIMOTHY   I rarely stay past the hour.

JIM   That's not true, you say that but that's not true.

TIMOTHY   Well, I don't wear a watch.

JIM   I do.

TIMOTHY   I know. I rely on you.

JIM   …

TIMOTHY   See you tomorrow.

JIM   You know it.

TIMOTHY goes.

2

Tuesday.

TIMOTHY and JIM at the crosswalk.

The light changes. JIM holds up his stop sign. He crosses the street and TIMOTHY crosses with him.

TIMOTHY   How's life?

JIM   Can't complain.

TIMOTHY   I'm sure you could.

JIM   Why go to the trouble.

TIMOTHY   Pigeons, still?

JIM   The second most reliable thing in my life. How're your parents?

TIMOTHY   Old.

JIM   Horrible way to be, old.

TIMOTHY   Is it?

JIM   How should I know?

JIM grips his jaw. He wriggles it, grimaces.

I lost a filling. It seems to have fallen out.

TIMOTHY   Is it causing you pain?

JIM   Not a whole lot. There's pain. Yeah, some. Mostly when
               I speak.

TIMOTHY   Maybe we shouldn't talk today then.

JIM   There's also pain when I don't speak.

TIMOTHY   Where the filling was?

JIM   This hurts too much. Can we cross please?

TIMOTHY   Okay.

                              They cross.

JIM   So what are your plans like? Have you made plans?

TIMOTHY   Plans for what.

JIM   For when you graduate. You thought at all about uni-
               versity, college?

TIMOTHY   I haven't thought about it much.

JIM   Huh. I'd imagine it'd be on your mind.

TIMOTHY   It's not.

JIM   Would you stay here?

TIMOTHY   Who knows.

JIM   Seems foolish to me, to sacrifice your life for the sake
               of a ritual.

TIMOTHY   It's not a ritual.

JIM   Then what is it.

TIMOTHY   It's a routine.

JIM   Whatever you say.

TIMOTHY   I don't even know if I'd recognize her.

JIM   Maybe not.

TIMOTHY   She'd be older.

JIM   You're older too.

TIMOTHY   Not that much.

JIM   You're much older.

TIMOTHY   I don't feel all that different.

JIM   A significant part of your life has passed you by.

TIMOTHY   I didn't *miss* it. I mean, I was *there*.

JIM   Were you?

TIMOTHY   It's just that there's so much I have to tell her.

JIM   Like what. What would you tell her. You can tell me instead.

TIMOTHY   I'd want her to look at me.

JIM   You'd hope she'd be impressed with you?

TIMOTHY   No. No, not at all. That's not it at all. Why would she be impressed with me? Why would you say that. What time is it.

JIM   Four thirty.

TIMOTHY   No. Really? I'm such an idiot. Why'd you let me stay so long? It's embarrassing.

JIM   You should buy a watch.

TIMOTHY   I have a watch.

JIM   So? Wear it.

TIMOTHY   I don't like to wear it.

JIM   Why not?

TIMOTHY   It tells me what time it is. Can we cross?

JIM   I'm not in the mood.

TIMOTHY   We always used to be in sync.

JIM   Times change.

TIMOTHY   We always used to cross naturally, without talking about it.

JIM   I'm getting older.

TIMOTHY   That's your excuse for everything.

JIM   You're getting older too.

Timothy	Yeah yeah yeah.
Jim	It's not the same as when you were ten. It makes less sense now.
Timothy	Nothing's changed since then.
Jim	Well, I'll see you.

He starts to go.

Timothy	Wait. What? You can't leave first.
Jim	My shift is over.
Timothy	You never leave first.
Jim	You stayed later. My shift is over. What am I supposed to do, stand around here all day and all night? I'm a busy guy.
Timothy	No you're not.
Jim	Nevertheless.
Timothy	Come back!
Jim	See you, Timothy.
Timothy	This is all wrong!

Jim's gone.

Timothy stands there by himself. He waits a moment. Then he turns and heads home, bewildered.

3

Wednesday.

TIMOTHY at the crosswalk.

JIM's not there.

Instead there's a young woman in her mid-twenties, MIRIAM. She holds a crossing guard's stop sign. She wears a crossing guard's vest.

He stares at her.

MIRIAM   Are you crossing?

TIMOTHY   …

MIRIAM   We can cross now if you want.

TIMOTHY   …

MIRIAM   Your nose is running.

TIMOTHY   …

Without taking his eyes from her, he pulls a Kleenex from his pocket and blows his nose violently.

MIRIAM   Is your name Timothy?

TIMOTHY   …

MIRIAM   Is it?

TIMOTHY	…
MIRIAM	Are you all right?
TIMOTHY	…
MIRIAM	Are you—
TIMOTHY	Yes.
MIRIAM	What?
TIMOTHY	It's me.
MIRIAM	You.
TIMOTHY	Timothy.
MIRIAM	Right.
TIMOTHY	Jeannie.
MIRIAM	…
TIMOTHY	Jeannie.
MIRIAM	…
TIMOTHY	Jeannie?
MIRIAM	…Miriam.
TIMOTHY	…
MIRIAM	Hi.

TIMOTHY ...

MIRIAM Sorry.

TIMOTHY Who are you.

MIRIAM I'm Miriam.

TIMOTHY Yeah I got that. What are you doing here.

MIRIAM I volunteer.

TIMOTHY Where's Jim.

MIRIAM Sick. I usually do this over at Thornridge. They asked me to cover for him.

TIMOTHY How'd you know my name.

MIRIAM You're sort of famous.

TIMOTHY Me.

MIRIAM You come up at our crossing guard meetings.

TIMOTHY You have meetings.

MIRIAM We have lots of meetings. Mostly they're for complaining. The volunteers, the retirees especially, they have a lot of anger.

TIMOTHY Oh.

MIRIAM You're well-known among us. Jim speaks highly of you. I think it's really sweet.

TIMOTHY	Yeah, Jim's great.
MIRIAM	No, I mean your... this thing you do.
TIMOTHY	It's not really a... it's just sort of a... gesture, I'm not really... I mean I'm not really waiting, it's not like I really expect she's going to... how much did Jim say exactly?
MIRIAM	Your sister disappeared when you were ten. She told you to wait for her here. So you do, every school day. The way you've done for the last seven years. Is there more?
TIMOTHY	No, that's more or less...
MIRIAM	It's really something.
TIMOTHY	You're pretty young to be a crossing guard.
MIRIAM	Yeah, they're mostly retirees.
TIMOTHY	Is that awkward?
MIRIAM	I enjoy it. I've had the time, since my kids have been in school. And this way I can make sure they get across the road safely.
TIMOTHY	You have kids.
MIRIAM	One of each.
TIMOTHY	Pretty young for that too.
MIRIAM	If you think I'm young, you should see my kids.

TIMOTHY   Fair. Can we cross please?

MIRIAM   Why?

TIMOTHY   That's what we do.

MIRIAM   But you're waiting for your sister.

TIMOTHY   Yeah.

MIRIAM   So you don't actually need to get to the other side.

TIMOTHY   Not actually, no.

MIRIAM   It's better if I stay on this side.

TIMOTHY   Is it.

MIRIAM   Much.

TIMOTHY   …

MIRIAM   I don't tell you how to do your job.

TIMOTHY   I don't have a job.

MIRIAM   I don't tell you to get one.

TIMOTHY   We just met.

MIRIAM   How long do you wait here exactly?

TIMOTHY   Oh come on! You don't know *anything*.

            He walks away.

4

Thursday.

TIMOTHY with a phone book. He flips the pages. He stops. He writes down an address.

JIM at home, alone in his darkened living room. There's a knock at the door, offstage. He opens his eyes. The door opens, TIMOTHY enters. Silence.

JIM   Myrna? Did you let this boy in?

              No response.

              Did you bring me anything? Eh? You bring me some chicken soup? Chocolates?

TIMOTHY   No.

JIM   Pretty lousy, go breaking in on a sick guy and not bring anything.

TIMOTHY   Sorry.

JIM   How's the cold?

TIMOTHY   Terrible.

JIM   You look good.

TIMOTHY   It's just your angle.

JIM   What's the big idea.

TIMOTHY	…
JIM	Can I offer you some cake?
TIMOTHY	I didn't bring anything for you.
JIM	Who am I to hold a grudge.
TIMOTHY	I'm not hungry.
JIM	Thirsty?
TIMOTHY	I'm okay, thanks.
JIM	What's the big idea.
TIMOTHY	…
JIM	What, you think I'm dying? Man doesn't show up for work one day of his life, one solitary day, you think he's dying?
TIMOTHY	…
JIM	There used to be corn all the way up here. There never used to be children, houses, schools. It was all corn. Corn and wind. No city north of the highway. We'd take our bikes. Spend an afternoon. The hills. God, the hills, gearing down, the hills would take the breath right out of us.
TIMOTHY	…
JIM	Let's build a house, she said. Let's build a house and fill it with children.

TIMOTHY   …

JIM   That was years ago. I can't hardly remember how many years ago that was.

TIMOTHY   …

             JIM's eyes close.

             Jim?

JIM   …

TIMOTHY   Hey. Jim.

JIM   Just resting my eyes.

TIMOTHY   …

JIM   I've been going in and out. All day yesterday. And today. In and out. Drifting. Don't get too close.

TIMOTHY   I'm sick already.

JIM   No you're not.

TIMOTHY   …

JIM   There was a close call once, at the crosswalk, just before you started coming. You know that? A girl almost died on my watch. She started crossing without me. She was struck by a car. "Oh my God, oh my God," the man said, the driver. "What have I done," the man said. But I didn't feel that way about it. I didn't feel that way at all. I might've told him. "Sir," I might've said. "Sir, I think you've misunderstood the situation." But I didn't say a thing. I stood on the corner. I held my sign. I watched him. "What have I done," the man said.

TIMOTHY   When was this?

JIM   Oh, before. A long time ago. I'd just started.

TIMOTHY   Did the girl die?

JIM   What time is it.

TIMOTHY   Almost noon.

JIM   Why aren't you in school.

TIMOTHY   I came to visit you.

JIM   You should be in school.

TIMOTHY   Maybe.

JIM   And if I died, would you keep waiting there still?

TIMOTHY   …

JIM   If I died? Eh? If I didn't show up because I was dead? What then.

TIMOTHY   I don't know.

JIM   Give it up.

TIMOTHY   I should probably head over to school—

JIM   Give it up. Get on with your life. Go figure out what kind of man you might be. Give it up.

23

TIMOTHY   I'll get my mom to make you some food, okay? I'll bring it over after—

JIM   You listen to me.

TIMOTHY   …It's just that it's been so long. I've been standing there for so long I don't know how I'd stop. Because on any given day there's as much or as little reason to stop as there was on the day before, when I didn't. When I stood there, as always. There'd have to be a reason. I couldn't just stop waiting for no reason.

JIM   What kind of reason do you need.

TIMOTHY   If she showed up. That would be a reason.

JIM   And if I died.

TIMOTHY   Why would you die?

JIM   But if I died. Would that be a reason.

TIMOTHY   I don't know.

JIM   I guess that would depend on whether you come for her or for me.

TIMOTHY   …

JIM   I'm there. She's not.

TIMOTHY   …

JIM   I'm old, Timothy.

TIMOTHY   I don't know what that means.

JIM   Look at my face.

TIMOTHY   It looks like mine.

JIM   Are you on drugs.

TIMOTHY   You have eyes, a mouth. I've never felt young.

JIM   Go to school.

TIMOTHY   Why would you die.

JIM   The wind's too loud at night. Go to school.

5

Friday.

TIMOTHY and MIRIAM at the crosswalk. She's wearing her vest and holding her stop sign.

TIMOTHY   How's life?

MIRIAM   I'm kind of an insomniac.

TIMOTHY   Oh.

MIRIAM   You?

TIMOTHY   Can't complain. How're the kids?

MIRIAM   Tiring.

TIMOTHY   I imagine.

MIRIAM   Can you?

TIMOTHY   Not really. Can we cross?

MIRIAM   I thought we went over this the last time.

TIMOTHY   …

MIRIAM   So explain something to me. You were really close with
               your sister, is that it? You had an unusual sort of bond?

TIMOTHY   I don't like to talk about it.

MIRIAM   I'm interested though, I mean I'm not trying to be a
               jerk, I'm genuinely interested, I find it moving that
               you'd—

TIMOTHY   I don't think it's really worth—

MIRIAM   No, but I'm moved by you, I've given it some thought
               and really—

TIMOTHY   I guess we were pretty close.

MIRIAM   I wish I'd had that kind of closeness with somebody
               growing up.

TIMOTHY   But there were seven years between us, we were at very
               different stages of… so we were close, yeah, but…

MIRIAM   …

TIMOTHY   I relied on her. I was the younger brother, I depended
               on her, I counted on her, but… I don't have any reason

26

to believe that it was mutual, reciprocal... you know? It's not like she relied on me too. I was ten.

MIRIAM   But to come every day, to wait...

TIMOTHY   But it's not really waiting, it's more...

MIRIAM   It's not.

TIMOTHY   No, like I said, there's no expectation, it's a routine, it's something I do, it makes sense to me, and Jim's here.

MIRIAM   ...

TIMOTHY   I don't know. Really. I don't know. I don't like to talk about it. I just started doing it. I kept doing it. I keep doing it. What's the problem? You have a problem with it? I don't understand why I have to defend what I choose to—

MIRIAM   You don't have to defend anything, I was only—

TIMOTHY   And I don't like that you don't like to cross the street, that you stay in the same spot, which means that I have to stay in the same spot, on the same side, which defeats the purpose, which really detracts from my whole sense of being here, and I don't like it, okay, I don't like it.

MIRIAM   Do you want to cross the street?

TIMOTHY   No, no I don't. No. No I don't.

MIRIAM   ...

TIMOTHY   ...

MIRIAM   Do you want to go to a movie with me tomorrow?

TIMOTHY   What?

MIRIAM   Tomorrow. You know, Saturday. Like in the evening. Do you want to?

TIMOTHY   What?

MIRIAM   A movie.

TIMOTHY   Oh. What? Oh. What movie do you want to see?

MIRIAM   Doesn't matter much to me.

TIMOTHY   Me neither.

MIRIAM   So it's a plan.

TIMOTHY   It's… sure. Sure.

MIRIAM   Just as friends.

TIMOTHY   Obviously. I mean you've got kids.

MIRIAM   Let me give you my number.

            He takes his cellphone out of his pocket, flips it open, hands it to her. She puts her number in his phone and gives it back to him.

TIMOTHY   I don't see a lot of movies.

MIRIAM   No?

TIMOTHY   I think if I had more friends I'd probably see more movies.

MIRIAM   Why don't you have more friends?

TIMOTHY   When's Jim coming back.

MIRIAM   …You must know. You do know, don't you?

TIMOTHY   Know what.

MIRIAM   He's sick.

TIMOTHY   Yeah, sure. You're covering for him.

MIRIAM   No, I mean it's really advanced.

TIMOTHY   Advanced?

MIRIAM   It's terminal.

TIMOTHY   What?

MIRIAM   You didn't know?

TIMOTHY   …

MIRIAM   I'm sorry.

TIMOTHY   …

MIRIAM   I don't think he plans to come back. That was the feeling at the meeting. He enjoys it but it's gotten too hard for him. He's pretty much confined to his bed at this point.

TIMOTHY   …

MIRIAM   You really didn't know?

TIMOTHY   But he seemed fine. But he looked totally fine.

MIRIAM   Supposedly he's on a lot of pills.

TIMOTHY   But he looked totally fine.

MIRIAM   …

TIMOTHY   What time is it.

MIRIAM   Twelve past four.

TIMOTHY   Good enough.

                  He walks away.

MIRIAM   Hey! So are we still on for tomorrow?

6

Saturday. Early morning.

JIM in his darkened living room. Morning light streams through gaps in the window blinds.

There's a knocking at the front door of the house.

He opens his eyes. He listens.

The knocking again.

He frowns.

JIM No, you were right all along. We should've adopted one. The silence in the house, it was unseemly, it was offensive. You were right. What was it? Vanity. God, yes. I wanted to have one that looked like me. I wanted one who'd know me by instinct. Vanity.

Knocking.

Who could that be? So early. What day is it? Timothy? Myrna, is it... no, never mind. Just pay it no mind. Tell him I'm not here. I'm not here. I'm going back to sleep now.

He closes his eyes. He opens them.

Maybe there was a silly sort of longing in it. They stood on one bank. And waited for the sea to part. I brought them dryly over. Left the terrors behind them on the shore, to languish or to drown. Maybe there was a silly sort of longing. Their faces. Sleepy morning faces. I never met their eyes. But so what about that, anyway. I did my part and did it well enough.

Knocking.

Who could that be? What time is it? Who'd come so early? Myrna, is it the boy again? Tell him I'm still sleeping. Or give him some cake. I think there's a little left of the cake I made on Wednesday. Invite him in. I'll be there soon.

The knocking stops. Silence.

Yes, I'll be there soon. I know I'm needed.

He frowns. He doesn't move.

31

7

Saturday night.

TIMOTHY at the crosswalk. He's sitting on the curb. Around him street lamps glow.

MIRIAM walks up wearing a knapsack. She waves. He waves back.

MIRIAM   Glad you called.

TIMOTHY   Glad you answered.

MIRIAM   This was a good idea. Going to the movies is anti-social anyway.

TIMOTHY   So you want to walk out to the park or something?

MIRIAM   Nah, here's good. Better lit.

             She unzips her knapsack, pulls out a picnic blanket, spreads it on the grass between the sidewalk and the road.

TIMOTHY   A sidewalk picnic?

             She pulls out a loaf of bread, a jar filled with something dark and shimmering, an unlabelled wine bottle filled with clear liquid, and two plastic cups. She uncorks the bottle and pours two drinks. She hands him one.

             What is it?

MIRIAM   Homemade wine. My husband's brother makes it.

TIMOTHY   Your husband?

MIRIAM   Sure. Two kids, remember.

TIMOTHY   Yeah, but I wasn't sure if... it's just that you're so young.

MIRIAM   I was impatient. I didn't know how long I'd live.

TIMOTHY   Why, were you sick?

MIRIAM   No. Why? Do you know how long you'll live?

TIMOTHY   ...What's this?

                He points at the jar.

MIRIAM   Honey.

TIMOTHY   Why honey?

MIRIAM   For the bread.

TIMOTHY   Okay, why bread?

MIRIAM   You can't just scoop up honey with your fingers.

                *She unwraps the bread, unscrews the jar's cap, dips a
                slice of bread in the honey and hands it to him. He
                bites. She takes a slice for herself, dips it, bites. They
                drink, they eat. They look out at the street.*

Once, when I was a very little girl, my mother left a
slice of bread and honey on a plate in our front yard.
We'd been sitting out there, watching my brothers play
basketball, and then we'd gone inside and forgotten
the plate. All of a sudden I hear my mother shouting

to us from the front of the house. "Come quick, come quick," she's shouting, "come quick or you'll miss it." So we all come to the front of the house, and she's in the living room, by the window, and she points, she says "Look, look." We look. It's a peacock. A peacock, in our yard. It's just standing there, where the bread was. Deep blues, emerald greens. Shimmering in the sunlight. Turquoise ovals in its plume like a hundred eyes. We pressed our faces to the window. It stayed nearly an hour. We just stared and stared. Nobody would even move to get the camera. "It ate the bread," my mother says. "Look at that, it ate the bread."

TIMOTHY finishes a slice, drinks.

Tell me about your sister.

TIMOTHY   …

MIRIAM   What did she look like?

TIMOTHY   …I don't really remember.

MIRIAM   Really?

TIMOTHY   Yeah. Nope. My parents put the pictures away. And I stopped looking at the few I stole.

MIRIAM   Why?

TIMOTHY   I couldn't handle her looking younger than me. I was the younger brother.

MIRIAM   You could be anything you want, you know.

TIMOTHY   You don't know anything about me.

MIRIAM   You're young. You've got a clear head. You start a thing
                and you stick to it. It bothers me to see you losing so
                much time on—

TIMOTHY   What's it to you. You have no reason to care. You don't
                know me at all.

MIRIAM   It's an instinct. It's unreasonable. Do you want me to
                cut it out?

TIMOTHY   …

MIRIAM   I've never understood talk about excessive grief. Grief's
                an instinct too, isn't it? It's only excessive if it's not in-
                stinctive, if it's pushed. If it's a crutch.

TIMOTHY   I went to Jim's house this morning. I knocked on his
                door, I waited a minute, I ran away. That's me. That's
                how I'm equipped.

MIRIAM   So?

TIMOTHY   How exactly am I supposed to survive?

MIRIAM   Who knows.

TIMOTHY   Who knows?

MIRIAM   I sure don't. Try hard?

                He drinks.

TIMOTHY   It's just that if I stopped coming all at once… I mean if
                one day I just didn't show up, after seven years, it'd…
                but no, because then the whole time I wasn't there I'd be
                thinking about it, about her, about Jim… and even if…

35

MIRIAM   You could stop gradually.

TIMOTHY   Yeah, yeah, that's what I was going to… because even if
            one day I just didn't show up, I couldn't just not show
            up the next day, I'd have to stagger it, I'd have to do it
            in a sort of progression, so that maybe I'd get it down to
            three times a week, and then twice a week, and then…
            but maybe it'd be harder that way, maybe it'd be easier
            just to, you know, like a Band-Aid… but I couldn't do
            that, it's not so simple, it's not just me who's affected
            by this…

MIRIAM   Who else?

TIMOTHY   Jim, obviously. He depends on me. It'd break his heart.

MIRIAM   I don't understand. Why would it break Jim's heart?
            He's not there.

TIMOTHY   …

MIRIAM   He's sick. He's not coming anymore. He won't know
            whether you're there or not.

TIMOTHY   …

MIRIAM   Why don't you just try it. Skip a day. See what happens.

            *He dips a piece of bread in honey and holds it up to
            the lightfall of the street lamp. He stares at it. It glows.*

            So eat it already.

            He does.

TIMOTHY   I've never seen a peacock before. Think I've seen photographs. But I can't picture one. What does it look like?

MIRIAM   Like something that should either be immortal or extinct.

TIMOTHY   What if the world is terrible.

MIRIAM   …

TIMOTHY   Of course I realize it's not safe here either. Terrible things happen here too. Nowhere's safe.

> *He stares out at the street. She puts the wine bottle, cups, bread and blanket into her knapsack and gets up.*

You're leaving me?

MIRIAM   Goodbyes need privacy. I'm in the way.

TIMOTHY   Wait.

MIRIAM   Feel free to call me.

> *She goes. She's forgotten her jar of honey.*
>
> *For a long moment he sits there by himself, watching the street, not moving.*
>
> *Then, slowly and decisively, he takes the jar, gets up and walks away.*

8

Monday.

MIRIAM at the crosswalk, wearing her vest and holding her stop sign.

TIMOTHY's not there.

JIM approaches, wearing his vest and holding his stop sign.

JIM   Good afternoon, Miriam.

MIRIAM   Hi Jim.

JIM   They didn't call you? I told them I was coming back today.

MIRIAM   No, nobody called me. How are you feeling?

JIM   Like a seventeen-year-old boy.

MIRIAM   God forbid.

JIM   How're yours?

MIRIAM   Healthy.

JIM   Wonderful.

MIRIAM   I'm surprised... well, it's none of my business. But I'm surprised you didn't tell him.

JIM   Tell who what.

MIRIAM   Your friend.

JIM   Who, Timothy? Tell him what.

MIRIAM   …

JIM   I've never felt better. I've never felt better in all my life.

MIRIAM   …

JIM   Wonder where he is. He's late. He's never late.

MIRIAM   I think there's a chance he may not be coming today.

JIM   Impossible.

MIRIAM   I think there's even a strong chance. A probability.

JIM   He's never missed a day. Even in blizzards, when the school shut down. He bundled up. He's just late.

MIRIAM   Sooner or later he's bound to stop coming.

JIM   Of course he is.

MIRIAM   He'll grow up, move on.

JIM   Of course he will.

MIRIAM   It'll be the best thing for him. Don't you think?

JIM   Of course. Why wouldn't I? I've told him that. You don't think I've told him that? Why wouldn't I want what's best for him?

MIRIAM   …

JIM   He's never been this late. Go on why don't you. Let
             me handle this. I'm all right here. I've been doing this
             for nearly a dozen years. I've been doing this since you
             were still a student here. I helped you across. I know
             what I'm doing. Go on.

MIRIAM   You're sure you're okay.

JIM   Look at my shining face. How can you even ask.

MIRIAM   I'll call the office, let them know you're back.

JIM   You call the office. You do that. The air is full of mois-
             ture. Everything is in bloom. Go on, I'm fine here. I've
             got my sign.

MIRIAM   Take care of yourself, Jim.

JIM   Sure I will. Go on now.

             She goes.

             *He stands at the crosswalk, sign in hand. He stares
             at the street, at the school, at the kids milling in the
             playground beside it. A long silence.*

             *TIMOTHY approaches, the jar half full of honey in his
             hands. He sees JIM, sees JIM staring off.*

TIMOTHY   Jim.

             JIM turns. He sees TIMOTHY. He smiles.

JIM   I knew you'd turn up.

TIMOTHY   You're back.

JIM   Where would I go?

TIMOTHY I thought you…

JIM   Nothing could keep me away. It's my routine.

TIMOTHY How're you feeling?

JIM   Couldn't be better. How's your cold?

TIMOTHY Not a big deal.

JIM   Glad you came.

TIMOTHY I only came to give back this jar, the girl who was fill-ing in for you left it and I thought I'd find her here, otherwise I decided I…

JIM   No matter, no matter: you came. Put it down a second.

      TIMOTHY puts down the jar. JIM starts to unfasten his vest.

TIMOTHY What are you doing?

      JIM places his sign between his knees, pulls off his vest and moves around behind TIMOTHY.

JIM   I'm retiring.

      He puts TIMOTHY's arms through the armholes of the vest. He reaches around him and fastens it up the front. He smiles.

      I'm moving on. Just wanted to come and pass the torch. You're always here. You don't want to leave. Good: so

41

you'll stay here. Me, I'm going to go and live my life. Take the sign.

TIMOTHY   …

       He holds it out. TIMOTHY stares at it.

JIM   Take the sign.

TIMOTHY   …

       He holds it out. TIMOTHY stares at it.

JIM   Please take the sign.

TIMOTHY   …

       TIMOTHY takes the sign.

    But I only came to…

JIM   Hold it up.

TIMOTHY   I wasn't going to come anymore…

JIM   Like this. So the cars can see it.

TIMOTHY   I decided I… I'm over it… I'm done… I'm not going to come anymore…

JIM   What a relief: your turn now—God! The air is full of moisture, everything's in bloom. I can be anything I want. Shall we cross? Let's cross.

TIMOTHY   But the light's not…

JIM's not listening. Smiling, he walks into the road. TIMOTHY opens his mouth. No sound comes out.

A long blast of a car horn. A screech of brakes. A clunk.

TIMOTHY stands at the crosswalk, wearing JIM's vest, holding JIM's stop sign. He stares out at the road. He doesn't move.

IN FULL LIGHT

In Full Light was first presented by Tango Co. on August 3, 2007, as part of the 2007 SummerWorks Theatre Festival, Toronto, in the Tarragon Theatre Mainspace, with the following cast and crew:

Claire: Monica Dottor
Leon: David Ferry
Ben: Tom Barnett
Lola: Gina Wilkinson
Marshall: Brendan Gall

Director and designer: Natasha Mytnowych
Lighting: André du Toit and Natasha Mytnowych
Sound and music: Lyon Smith
Costumes: Naomi Skwarna
Choreography: Monica Dottor
Stage managers: Jennifer Dowding and Joy Lachica

In Full Light was the recipient of the 2007 SummerWorks Festival's Contra Guys Award for Outstanding New Play. It was developed in part through the Canadian Stage Play Development Program with dramaturg Iris Turcott. It was subsequently presented as part of the hotINK Festival at the Rita and Burton Goldberg Theatre, New York, directed by Linsay Firman, in January 2009. The Hans Otto Theater in Potsdam, Germany, produced a translation of the play by Barbara Christ as *Weiss wie das Licht*, directed by Marc Lunghuss, as part of the 2009/2010 season.

CHARACTERS (IN ORDER OF APPEARANCE)

Claire, fifteen
Leon, forty-five
Ben, forty-two, Claire's father
Lola, thirty-eight, Ben's wife
Marshall, nineteen, who lives across the street

NOTE

An ellipsis (…) appearing on its own or before a line of dialogue indicates a silent, momentary response to what has just been said or not said.

A slash (/) indicates a point at which the following line cuts in early, creating overlap.

Then a few things will follow
from these first conditions: women
singing in full light and at dusk
before reflecting water;
and some way to live together
that is not a scandal and a shame.
—A. F. Moritz, "What They Prayed For"

A rush of air. A screech of brakes. CLAIRE is splayed out violently, unnaturally, in the middle of the road. She's still. Watching her, around her, are BEN, LOLA, MARSHALL and LEON. Each of them is isolated, alone. CLAIRE shifts. She shifts again. Is she injured or is she posing?

CLAIRE   How should I be? Like this?

As though both arms were broken.

Or like this?

Tongue out, fingers up her nose, legs twisted out of place.

Oh fuck me! So ridiculous, I'm dying, I'm gonna die, like for sure, probably, and all I can think about is whether you thought I was beautiful when I flew up the windshield.

LEON is in distress. BEN turns to him.

LEON   I can't even begin to understand—

BEN   So what happened, she / just—

LEON   Just stopped walking all of a sudden in the middle of the street, I slammed on my brakes, I wasn't really even going that fast but I guess—are you all right?

BEN	I'm fine, finish what you're saying.
LEON	I'm really so sorry, I can't tell you—
BEN	Finish what you're saying.
LEON	No, please, listen to me, I'm really a low shit, making excuses for myself right after I've, I've—I'm sure you don't want to chit-chat with me. I'm sure you'd rather hit me.
BEN	Hit you? I don't want to hit you.
LEON	I would want to. In your position. Somebody hurt my daughter, I'd want to hit him.

LOLA places a hand on BEN's shoulder. BEN turns to her. LEON is gone.

LOLA	So did you?
BEN	Excuse me?
LOLA	Did you hit him.
BEN	Are you kidding? No. No, of course I didn't hit him. Why would I hit him?

CLAIRE is in the hospital. The beep of a monitor.

CLAIRE	Invisibility. Absolute invisibility. It's the only explanation. My dad comes into the room, he sits beside the bed, he talks to himself, he gets up and leaves. He doesn't see me. He can kiss me on the cheek without seeing me. And all these doctors buzzing around, calling my name but not meaning me by it—can they see me? Maybe they're blind, all these blind doctors moving

blindly through this hospital where all the patients can see. And you—would you be able to see me if you were here? Why aren't you here? Haven't you heard?

LOLA is on MARSHALL's front porch.

MARSHALL   Heard what?

LOLA   She was hit by a car.

MARSHALL   Oh. I mean yeah. I know. I mean I knew. Before just now.

LOLA   You did. Good. And so I was wondering, you're always at your window there, doing your bird thing—

MARSHALL   Oh not *always*, just, like, sometimes—

LOLA   And we've been trying to figure out how exactly this terrible thing happened, how she managed to get herself—

MARSHALL   You want to know if I saw it?

LOLA   Did you see it?

MARSHALL   What's it worth to you?

LOLA   …

MARSHALL   Kidding. I'm kidding, that's a joke, I'm sorry, I, uh, I guess this isn't the right time, is it? Yeah. Yes. I'll be serious now.

LOLA   I'm not sure what it's worth to me. Why don't you tell me first and then we can work something out?

MARSHALL   …Where's, uh… where's… your husband?

LOLA   At the hospital.

MARSHALL   …Yeah. Um. So like. What you wanted to… know. She ran out into the road. She stopped. He kept going. He hit her. He got out of his car, he pulled out his cell-phone, he called the ambulance. Ambulance arrived, ambulance left, he went with. That's all I saw.

LOLA   Thanks.

MARSHALL   Please.

LOLA   I hope you're still drawing.

MARSHALL   Oh. Yes. I am. Sometimes. It's cyclical. But I have to waste eight or nine hours for every hour of work I get done.

LOLA   Well. I'm sorry to interrupt your procrastination.

MARSHALL   Oh. No. You're… welcome.

LOLA   …

MARSHALL   Do you / wanna—?

LOLA   I'd better / go.

MARSHALL   Yeah. Yes.

LOLA   Take / care.

MARSHALL   And you.

Claire is in the hospital, Ben seated beside her.

CLAIRE   …Did he say he was sorry?

BEN   …He said he was sorry.

CLAIRE   …So…

BEN   …So… I'm not sure… the important… the most important thing is that you get better…

CLAIRE   …Yeah.

BEN   …I'm going to… I'm not sure exactly.

CLAIRE   You don't need to sue him or get him arrested or anything, Daddy.

BEN   He wasn't drinking.

CLAIRE   You don't have to do anything. It's okay.

BEN   It was an accident. And… you know I feel… but it was an / accident.

CLAIRE   I feel better already.

          Leon appears, leads Ben away. A reception area in the hospital.

LEON   That's good to hear, I mean jeez, I've just been thinking and thinking about it, how can you stop, you know, but I didn't think it was the proper thing to go up to her room and express my contrition if you can understand / where I'm coming from—

BEN	Of course, no, I don't think that's / necessary—
LEON	But I do feel that her well-being is my—in a way I mean—my responsibility, or that, well, that this is my fault, I guess is the bottom of it, this is all my fault, and I'm not sleeping, that's not your problem of course but I can't sleep anymore, haven't been able to for two weeks now, so…
BEN	…
LEON	I feel the need to compensate you for the, the situation I've put you and your family in, and I feel like me sitting around saying "sorry, sorry" doesn't cut it.
BEN	Oh, well, that's, I appreciate that, but there's really no need to… what exactly are you talking about?
LEON	I wrote you a cheque.
BEN	…But you know that I can't—I mean I couldn't—because—that's very generous of you but I wouldn't want you to find yourself in financial… I would feel very awkward about…
LEON	You're worried I can't afford it?
BEN	Can you?
LEON	I'm not sleeping, Benjamin.
BEN	Just Ben is fine.
LEON	I want to sleep, Ben. I'm being straight with you. I want to feel okay again. I want to enjoy eating meals

again. When I shave in the morning I want to be able to look at myself in the mirror.

BEN   I'm not sure if money will change any of that.

LEON   Maybe not. You ever have insomnia, Ben?

BEN   …

LEON   What do you do? You can't sleep so you what, you get up, you go to the kitchen, mix yourself a drink—what do you drink, Scotch—you close your eyes. You sit on the couch, you watch the TV, you watch the coloured bars on stations that are out of service. What else? You take long walks in the street maybe, you walk in the shadows because you don't want to be seen but every time a car passes you hope it'll stop and a friend will get out, someone who'll be a comfort, someone you can trust.

BEN   This is a little besides the point, don't you think?

LEON   How's your marriage?

BEN   What?

LEON   Healthy? Yeah? I'm curious.

BEN   That's kind of a personal question, don't you—

LEON   I'm sorry, is that not—?

BEN   My marriage is fine, thanks.

LEON   I'm not married, myself.

BEN	Okay.
LEON	Is your wife Claire's mother?
BEN	Excuse me—?
LEON	I'm sorry, is that not a polite / question?
BEN	A polite—I guess that depends what you consider—I don't think—why would you ask that? No, my wife is not Claire's mother, Claire's mother is in Montreal.
LEON	Is that complicated?
BEN	Not really, no, but—sorry, you'll have to excuse me, but it's very strange for me to be talking about this with you, considering the, the circumstances of our…
LEON	Yeah, I guess—
BEN	So to be sitting here talking about my ex with you, I never talk about my ex, frankly I'd rather talk about crabs, and here we are—
LEON	You can't always choose when and how you make a friend.
BEN	I don't think I'm the type of person who makes a lot of friends.
LEON	I'm the same way. I've got a lot of respect for you, you know.
BEN	Okay. Thanks.
LEON	Got a lot of respect for your situation, what you do, you know what I'm driving at: you're a family man, you

live for people other than yourself, even when we're sitting here and I offer you this large sum of money I can see you thinking not just about yourself, like a lot of people would, but also your family, how will this help them, how will this change their respect for you, all that. I can see that.

BEN   I won't accept a handout from a stranger.

LEON   It's not a handout, it's reparations.

BEN   I'm thinking about it.

LEON   Don't think too much.

> *He fishes a folded cheque from his pocket and places it in BEN's hands.*

BEN   …That's a lot of money.

LEON   I do okay for myself.

BEN   What can I say? What should I say to you?

LEON   Don't say anything.

> *CLAIRE is at her bedroom window.*

CLAIRE   Ornithology. The study of birds. The study of watching. Waiting and watching. Eight a.m. Every morning.

> *MARSHALL comes to his window with binoculars and notepad. He and CLAIRE can't hear each other.*

I once heard you telling Lola:

MARSHALL   It's calming. Like—

CLAIRE   Watching people. It's like watching people in the early
           morning—

MARSHALL   Only with birds the whole thing is simpler, because
           when you watch people you think:

CLAIRE   I need to understand—

MARSHALL   To understand, just to understand, how does it feel to
           be the man who delivers the water for our cooler, how
           does it feel to be the woman carrying her baby to the
           clinic at dawn—?

CLAIRE   But with birds, watching birds—

MARSHALL   It's much simpler, because I accept that I will never
           know what it is to be a bird, so I don't feel that endless
           responsibility to understand why the thing that I'm
           watching does what it does, and I can just—

CLAIRE   Watch.

MARSHALL   And record what's beautiful on paper, neat and logical.

CLAIRE   You pretend you're oblivious.

MARSHALL   I never learned the real names of birds. I can recog-
           nize a robin, a hawk, maybe a seagull. The rest I've
           created names for myself. Johnny-of-the-afternoon.
           Blue-who-heads-to-the-sea.

CLAIRE   But I've been so *obvious*. You must know. You must
           know everything. But if you know, why do you just
           torture me like this?

MARSHALL   Long-who-kisses-lawns-and-leaves.Wide-wings-leaving-
                on-wind-tomorrow.

CLAIRE   One of these days I'm going to knock on your door
                and say something to you, and then we'll actually have
                spoken, and what're you gonna do then, huh? Will you
                confess everything, you love me too and have delayed
                so long because you're a horrible person but you want
                to be better and can I teach you to be a better person?
                Will you say that?

MARSHALL   A chart for each bird, patterns of behaviour, quirks,
                moments of strange beauty. Morley-who-sings-away-
                seagulls. Lola-who-comes-to-make-chit-chat.

CLAIRE   If you haven't come to see how I'm feeling by tomor-
                row I'm going to knock on your door and tell you.

MARSHALL   Claire-at-the-window-hiding.

CLAIRE   And if you can't see me I'll murder you invisibly.

MARSHALL   A chart for each bird, patterns of behaviour, quirks,
                moments of strange beauty.

CLAIRE   If you don't come by tomorrow. Tomorrow—

                *Suddenly there's an insistent knocking at the door.
                CLAIRE goes to the door, opens it. There's MARSHALL. A
                long moment. She's staring. Then she can't meet his eye.*

MARSHALL   …Oh hi.

CLAIRE   …

MARSHALL   Um. You were hit by a car.

CLAIRE	…Uh-huh.
MARSHALL	That's real bad news. Sorry.
CLAIRE	…Yeah sorry. Yeah. I mean yeah okay. Don't be sorry or anything.
MARSHALL	So, uh, you have my deepest, my most sincere, um…
CLAIRE	Yeah?
MARSHALL	Condolences?
CLAIRE	…Oh. Thanks. Okay bye.
MARSHALL	Claire?
CLAIRE	Yes?
MARSHALL	No, nothing, I just wanted to make sure I had your name right.
CLAIRE	Claire.
MARSHALL	Yeah, I know.
CLAIRE	You must be smart. And your name, it starts with like an *N* or an… *L*…?
MARSHALL	It's Marshall.
CLAIRE	Oh, okay. Does anyone ever call you "Fire Marshall"?
MARSHALL	All the time.
CLAIRE	My condolences.

MARSHALL   So you were in the hospital, huh?

CLAIRE   Yeah. The hospital for the sighted.

MARSHALL   Huh?

CLAIRE   I dunno. Yeah.

MARSHALL   So... that sucks.

CLAIRE   Yeah.

MARSHALL   ...

CLAIRE   Um, don't you have anywhere to be now, like aren't you in school or something?

MARSHALL   I graduated.

CLAIRE   University?

MARSHALL   It's June.

CLAIRE   So in June you get to just bum around and be a jerk.

MARSHALL   ...

CLAIRE   Hello?

MARSHALL   ...

CLAIRE   What is wrong with you?

LOLA comes up behind her.

LOLA   Claire, I can't find my blouse with the stripes.

CLAIRE	I ate it.
LOLA	Thanks, thanks for the help. Hi Marshall, how are you?
MARSHALL	I don't know.
LOLA	Sorry to hear that.
MARSHALL	Yeah. Yes. True. So… feel better.

He goes.

LOLA	That's a very nice-looking kid.
CLAIRE	Oh my God. Can you be even a little bit serious? I'd rather sleep with a pine tree.
LOLA	You shouldn't be sleeping with anyone.
CLAIRE	No, I don't know where your blouse is.
LOLA	Fine, fine, I've really gotta get—you don't hate me, do you?
CLAIRE	Not at all.
LOLA	Don't hate me. I'm really not worth hating.

BEN is in his office. The phone rings. He picks up.

BEN	Hello—?
LEON	Why should a chemist be so hard to reach, I ask myself.
BEN	Is this—? Who is this?

LEON   This is Leon, you don't recognize my voice?

BEN   Leon… from the—?

LEON   Sure, Leon, you know other Leons? Maybe you know
            other Leons but I'd imagine I might be quite a large
            figure in your thinking if you know what it is I'm
            saying—

BEN   Right, yes, Leon—so what is it, what's going on?

LEON   What does a chemist do exactly, is it dangerous? If you
            put the wrong thing in the wrong bottle, know what I
            mean, seems like it could be a real bad—

BEN   Leon, is there something you want to say to me—

LEON   I'm sorry, sorry, listen to me, I run off at the mouth,
            but I, look, I can't do it like this, we've gotta meet, can
            you meet me?

BEN   I'm at work, Leon.

LEON   Of course, well aren't I just a son of a bitch, I'll try you
            another time, sorry to have interrupted, really, I mean I
            shouldn't expect a guy to be always on call for me just
            because I know him a little, that's all right, that's all
            right, I'm fine, I'm okay, I'll try you later.

            He hangs up abruptly.

            *CLAIRE is at her bedroom window. She's scribbling
            on a piece of paper. Then she rips the paper up. And
            again. And again.*

CLAIRE   He knows everything.

65

MARSHALL is at his bedroom window. Binoculars.

He thinks because he's old and has those dark jeans he can do whatever the frig he wants. "So I heard you were hit by a car!" But you never said a word to me.

MARSHALL   She's seen me. She didn't / have to say—

CLAIRE   You didn't say *an-y-thing*—

MARSHALL   It was an accusation—each little tip of her hip that she does like that: pervert, weirdo, creep.

CLAIRE   You were thinking "She's pathetic, she's silly, she's ugly, and I have to make sure she *knows* that."

MARSHALL   I don't want to get any closer than this. We'd have nothing to say to each other. She's too happy. Too optimistic.

CLAIRE   And you want to kill me, your deepest, darkest de-sire (I *know* you) is to see me suffer at the teeth of wild animals who eat hair too and to see me fall from a poetic height and die. You wish no afterlife for me so that when I'm gone from the earth I'll be gone also from conception, from eternity, forever. That way I can't haunt you.

MARSHALL   I'm afraid of changing her.

CLAIRE   I am going to write the filthiest words for you, I am going to write you words so filthy, so awful, you'll think how horrible it is that people exist who can hate so much.

MARSHALL   I'm afraid of fouling something pure.

CLAIRE is writing.

CLAIRE   "You are going to roll in the filth of pigs who sweat and shit at the same time and the pigs are going to step on your face and then you'll be no less pretty but that's before the pigs *eat* you."

MARSHALL   No. Better like this. Dependable.

CLAIRE   "Tomorrow a big man is going to kick you in the balls and you'll say 'Why?' and then he'll kick you in the balls again and your balls will fall off and at this point you'll get the idea to run but then he'll hit you with a steel bar and you'll be only a little less pretty then but that's still before he *eats* you."

MARSHALL   Uncomplicated.

CLAIRE   "Suck my cock."

            The phone rings. We hear the others but see only CLAIRE. She picks up.

            ...Is it you?

LEON   ...Can I speak to Ben, please?

CLAIRE   Oh. Who's this?

LEON   Who's this? I'm a good friend.

CLAIRE   You've got the wrong number. My dad doesn't have friends.

LEON   ...

CLAIRE	Hang on, hang on. Dad! For you.
BEN	Hello?
LEON	Come outside.
BEN	Excuse me—who—Leon?
LEON	Come outside, Ben.
BEN	…Where are you?
LEON	It's an emergency. I wouldn't do this if it wasn't. Come outside.
BEN	Where are you, Leon?
LEON	I'm across the street from your house.

> *BEN and LEON stand on opposite sides of the street.
> LEON holds a small duffle bag.*

BEN	…Why didn't you knock?
LEON	…If your daughter…
BEN	…Listen, Leon. If you're in some kind of trouble I sympathize with you, but I don't want you bringing that here where my family—
LEON	The trouble is I don't have any money.

> *He crosses the street and meets BEN. BEN glances at
> his house. His windows.*

BEN	You don't have any money.

LEON   Yeah, that would be my problem, I'm broke. I have nothing.

BEN   But you told me you had a... I don't understand.

LEON   Neither do I, life is strange, you know? First thing I
                hit a girl with my truck, next thing I lose my job, but
                oh, whoopsie, I've just given away all my savings to
                someone I know fuck all / about, excuse me—

BEN   No excuse *me*, what?

LEON   Sure, you think I just happened to have six thousand
                dollars tucked under my bed in case of some crisis of
                conscience? *No*, Ben, and that's okay, I'm an adult, I can
                make decisions and live with them, but the problem is
                now I have *nothing*, no money, no job—

BEN   Hang on, hang on, wait, that money was all your
                savings?

LEON   I smashed the piggy bank.

BEN   But... but then I can't understand... no, but why would
                you—

LEON   Because I'm not a bad person, Ben. Because I think
                about people other than myself.

BEN   There's selfless and then there's ridiculous.

LEON   You find me ridiculous?

BEN   So what is it you want? You didn't call me up just to—

LEON   I don't like this new tone, Ben, guys can still be friends
                when things get difficult.

BEN   Leon, let me be clear, and I don't want to be rude and I don't want to hurt your feelings, but considering everything I don't think of us as friends in the way you mean. So… I'm sorry, I just…

LEON   Well. It's a shame you feel that way.

BEN   I want to be honest with you.

LEON   You're very honest, I respect that about you.

BEN   Okay, so that's all we have to talk about, right? I'm sorry about your situation but—

LEON   The thing is I need the money back, Ben.

BEN   The money you gave me?

LEON   That's the only money there is.

BEN   But you… I don't feel comfortable with the idea that— but you gave it to me.

LEON   Yes, I know, and now I need it back.

BEN   It's gone.

LEON   It's gone. Where has it gone? You spent six thousand dollars in two weeks?

BEN   It's gone. You gave it to me and I used it.

LEON   Only natural.

BEN   What did you expect me to do with it? You hand me a cheque, you *insist*—

LEON   I never insisted—

BEN   —you *insist* I take it, so that you can sleep at night. I take it, I spend it. You have no reason to be angry or surprised—

LEON   I'm not surprised, I'm not angry, I'm just *asking*. I'm asking you to do me a favour, I'm in need and I'm *asking*, I'm not demanding, I'm not shouting, I'm just asking you to remember that I wasn't a bad guy to you when I could've been—

BEN   That's entirely different—

LEON   —okay it's different, you're right, I'm just telling you where I'm at now and asking if you can help a guy out. I don't have anywhere to sleep. I don't have anywhere to sleep or anything to eat and I'm asking you to help a guy out.

BEN   …

LEON   You're just gonna walk back into your house? You're gonna walk back into your warm, comfortable house and leave me standing here?

BEN   …

LEON   I know I deserve it. I know that's what I deserve, man. Make no mistake.

BEN   …

LEON   I have nowhere to go, Ben. I have nowhere to sleep.

BEN   …

Leon	You have a couch?
Ben	Pardon me?
Leon	The money's gone, I understand, only natural, but if I could lay my bones on your couch for a few days that'd really help me lots.
Ben	I really don't think I... my family is there.
Leon	Just a few days, Ben. Just till I can get things straightened out. I'll figure out how to get hold of some cash. Just need a bit of time.
Ben	...I don't think I can.
Leon	...
Ben	Really. It's not a good idea. I'm sorry.
Leon	...
Ben	I'm sorry.

LEON turns and starts to walk slowly away. A moment.

...Hold on.

LEON stops.

...Just... but... but just for a few days.

Leon	That's it.
Ben	...And... and... absolutely no later than the end of the week.

LEON   Absolutely.

BEN   ...All right.

LEON   That's very generous of you, Ben.

BEN   ...Well. I wouldn't want to be the kind of guy who...

           Darkness falls around them. Soon we can see only
           MARSHALL, lighted in the window, CLAIRE's note in
           his hand.

LEON   You're exactly like me.

           LEON and LOLA are in the kitchen, LOLA holding a
           cup of coffee.

LOLA   Oh yeah?

LEON   No milk, no cream, a little sugar.

LOLA   Would you like a cup?

LEON   Oh no, just saying.

LOLA   Any luck with the paper, did you find anything?

LEON   Sure, sure, lots of jobs out there, trouble is I'm not re-
           ally qualified for anything. Spent most of my life in
           the merchant marine. Most of my working life. Signed
           up when I was fourteen. I'd seen more of the world at
           twenty-five than most people will see if they live to be
           a hundred. Six continents, all kinds of labour, manual
           labour. I've been kidnapped for ransom and held at
           gunpoint twice. I've known countless ports of call and
           the people in them. That's a hard-working, honest life.

LOLA	I think it's admirable that you've done things that excite you. The merchant marine sounds adventurous—
LEON	Yeah shit, excuse me, but that's a load of you know what. Adventure is what it is at seventeen. By twenty, make no mistake, it's work. Certainly there's no pride there for me now. Do you think I've told your husband that that's how I've spent the better part of my life?
LOLA	You haven't told Ben—?
LEON	No I did not tell your husband that I spent years and years in a community of men with a reputation for extreme misogyny and violence. No I did not.
LOLA	He's more compassionate than you think.
LEON	He would throw me out of your house. Politely, of course. But he would throw me out of your house. And he's right, that's exactly what he should do, because he's got you and his daughter here and he's got to think about you first. Your safety.
LOLA	That's really absurd, Leon.
LEON	Is it?
LOLA	…The merchant marine, huh? I've never met anyone before who's done that for a living. It was really that bad?
LEON	Well no, it wasn't bad, but like anywhere else you had a mix of honest men and men who'd take a knife to your hand in the night for the rings on your fingers. Often the same man contained both possibilities.

LOLA   I would never take a knife to your hand for the rings on your fingers. Neither would Ben. So you can sleep easy here.

LEON   Thanks. That's kind of you to say. But then you and Ben don't have any need of rings.

LOLA   We're honest besides.

LEON   Your husband married quite a remarkable woman.

LOLA   Yeah, his first wife. Anyway, if you're all right here I'm going to head out for a while—

LEON   No, I never married, myself.

LOLA   Too many ports of call?

LEON   Oh no, no. Just never married. I was engaged once.

LOLA   Uh-huh.

LEON   Oh yeah. Yeah, yeah. Once upon a time. It didn't work out.

LOLA   I'm sorry.

LEON   She decided I was too dependent.

LOLA   Were you?

LEON   It's good to be around people again, you know? You spend too much time alone, you begin to lose your bearings. My apartment wasn't very big. Even the windows were narrow.

LOLA You can also be alone in a bed you're sharing once the lights go out.

The lights go out.

It's nighttime. MARSHALL crosses to CLAIRE's house and leaves a slip of paper in the handle of her front door. CLAIRE snaps on her flashlight, leaves her house, retrieves and reads his note.

CLAIRE "You eat Chinese food? Maybe we should go eat Chinese food together. If you want. You know where I live. M."

She's still a moment. Then she rips his note into pieces, blows her nose with them and stomps them underfoot.

This is how the universe laughs at me. I tell him I love him, I use words that aren't as pretty and stuff but still I tell him, and he asks me if I want *Chinese food*? There is a name for that, that is *cruelty*. He could say no, I don't love you, but oh no!—he wants to cause me pain. Probably very few people make themselves vulnerable to him like that, so when he sees the opportunity, *wham*!—he grabs it. The fucking cunt-faced cocksucker son of a bitch.

With her flashlight she finds a large rock. She picks it up and shuffles it between her hands. It's not light.

Fuck with somebody else, asswipe.

She wings the rock into MARSHALL's bedroom window and runs back to the safety of her house as the window shatters.

MARSHALL wakes up. He sees the window in pieces. He stumbles forward and finds the rock among the shards. He picks it up, looks at it, tosses it back and forth between his hands. On his face is a look of pure wonder.

MARSHALL   Look at that. Look at that.

He's smiling like an ecstatic standing for the first time in holy light. He can't move.

No one has ever…

He stands in the window frame where the glass used to be. His face is a ghostly white in the moonlight.

CLAIRE returns to her house, closing the front door soundlessly. The beam of her flashlight catches on LEON's face. Startled, she makes a noise. Hastily she snaps the flashlight off. For a moment there's complete silence and darkness.

LEON   Sorry I scared you.

She snaps the flashlight back on. LEON is sitting alone in the living room. She approaches him, lights him. Sits down beside him. Their faces are lit by her flashlight beam.

CLAIRE   What are you doing?

LEON   Sitting.

CLAIRE   Just sitting?

LEON   Listening to the night. There was a crash.

CLAIRE	A cat knocked over a garbage can.
LEON	Sounded like glass breaking.
CLAIRE	There was glass inside the garbage can.
LEON	Why are you walking around with a flashlight?
CLAIRE	Hey, this is my house, I can do that if I want, okay?
LEON	You can do anything you want.
CLAIRE	Fucking right.
LEON	You're very polite.
CLAIRE	Love has made a monster of me.
LEON	Love.
CLAIRE	Love. You wouldn't know anything about it.
LEON	You think I've never been in love.
CLAIRE	Not the same kind. I mean a scratch his face, vomit in his shoes, throw his liver to the dogs kind of love. You can't touch that kind of love.
LEON	I once threw a woman I loved down a flight of stairs.
CLAIRE	…Really?
LEON	Sure.
CLAIRE	Why?

LEON	She stopped loving me. I still loved her.
CLAIRE	So what do you do to someone you hate?
LEON	...Sorry, sweetheart, I don't think I understand your question.
CLAIRE	...You don't make me feel safe at all.
LEON	Am I supposed to?
CLAIRE	You're old. Most old people do.
LEON	What would I have to do to make you feel safe?
CLAIRE	Not remind me of me.
LEON	It's late. Shouldn't you get a little sleep?
CLAIRE	We're not kind, people like us.
LEON	Speak for yourself. I'm a very kind person.
CLAIRE	I'm not a kind person. But I want to be. I think I do. I *want* to want to be.
LEON	Whoever told you it's to your advantage to be kind was lying through his teeth.
CLAIRE	Sooner or later he's going to throw you out of our house.
LEON	Maybe. But why do you think so?
CLAIRE	Because of the things that are in your head. I've seen you.

CLAIRE's flashlight snaps off. Darkness.

LOLA   Claire? Is that… oh. Hi. Can't sleep?

LEON   I rarely sleep.

         Sound of a window curtain pushed aside. Moonlight seeps in.

LOLA   You're welcome to turn on the TV…

LEON   Don't like late-night television. Thanks.

LOLA   Whatever you like. I just heard a noise and thought I'd better…

LEON   Lola.

LOLA   …Goodnight, Leon.

LEON   I try to live honestly.

LOLA   I know that, Leon. Hope you can get some sleep. I'll see you in the morning.

LEON   Wait.

LOLA   …

LEON   Wait.

LOLA   …

LEON   I want to tell you this outright, I don't want to play games, or, or do those things people do, I'm not interested. And I'm sorry to approach you like this, to back you into a corner such as it is, but I'm very afraid right now, and this is how I've got to do it, forgive me.

LOLA …You've been a guest in our home, Leon.

LEON I know that, I know, frankly I know exactly what you're going to say, and that's fine, that's just fine. I think you are a remarkable woman and truly and fully unappreciated where you are at this moment, and I look at your life and I think how sad that is, how boring it must be, how lonely. You're an outsider in your own house. Is this an accurate picture I'm painting?

LOLA …You don't understand.

LEON No, really I don't understand, I don't understand why a woman like you, beautiful, intelligent, why you go on this way, when you could be so much happier. What is it? Is it comfort that keeps you going like this, familiarity, routine—?

LOLA I don't have to explain myself to you.

LEON This is a simple request I have, just hear me out. I know it's dark and we're alone and that's a potentially uncomfortable position for you to be in, and me too. This is what I want to do. I want to put my hand in your hair. I may touch your face. That's all I want. If you're not interested in my idea I will respect that and leave you alone. I know you're a faithful wife, I wouldn't want to change that. I want only to make you aware of your options.

LOLA …

LEON You're not saying anything. That's fine. That's wise. You're guilty of nothing.

> *Tenderly he runs his hand through her hair. She
> flinches, pulls away. Again he places his hand in her
> hair. She flinches. But she doesn't pull away. He cups
> and strokes the side of her face.*

LOLA   Leon…

LEON   …Shh. Not necessary.

LOLA   …I'm not a weak person. You can't imagine what
           strength I have in me.

LEON   I won't kiss you unless you ask me to.

LOLA   I love my husband.

LEON   He's a very good man. I respect him very much.

LOLA   Clearly not.

LEON   I have tremendous admiration and respect for you. It
           saddens me that you have your eyes closed like this.
           You're afraid of loneliness. Okay. So am I. So is he. I
           can see all of you.

LOLA   My life is with my husband.

LEON   I won't kiss you unless in no uncertain terms you ask
           me to.

LOLA   I won't.

LEON   Then we can stand here like this all night and I'll be
           perfectly happy.

LOLA   …

LEON   So will you.

             She doesn't move.

             Elsewhere: a pebble raps against a window. And again. A light comes on. CLAIRE *looks out the window, goes to the front door, takes a breath and opens the door for* MARSHALL.

MARSHALL   So I got your message.

CLAIRE   …

MARSHALL   So I got your message—?

CLAIRE   I didn't send you a message.

MARSHALL   Oh. But like, it's—okay, fine, forget it.

CLAIRE   …

MARSHALL   So were you sleeping just now, or what—?

CLAIRE   It wasn't a message. It was a rock.

MARSHALL   Oh. Yeah I know.

CLAIRE   So listen, I'm sorry, okay? Are you gonna ask me to like pay for the—

MARSHALL   No, no, I just wanted to tell you that I appreciated it.

CLAIRE   Appreciated it how?

MARSHALL   Just… I dunno. Take it at face value.

CLAIRE   Oh. So… you're welcome?

MARSHALL   …So what's going on, like what were you doing just now when I came, like with your life I mean?

CLAIRE   It's three in the morning.

MARSHALL   Sure, sure, still.

CLAIRE   I was sleeping.

MARSHALL   Yeah okay. Sleeping. Right. But you're not sleeping anymore, so, uh, what do you wanna do?

CLAIRE   …

MARSHALL   I mean it's okay if you just want to go back to sleep. I can go home. I don't live far.

CLAIRE   You're making fun of me.

MARSHALL   What? No, no. I'm… I don't know, I'm talking.

CLAIRE   You're not fucking with my head?

MARSHALL   I don't think so.

CLAIRE   It's three in the morning and you're asking me what I want to do?

MARSHALL   Uh-huh, yeah, I think so.

CLAIRE   …I want to see my house.

MARSHALL   Turn around.

CLAIRE   I want to see my house like you see my house. I want
           to see my bedroom.

           A moment. He turns, motions for her to follow.
           They enter his house. His bedroom. They look out
           his window.

           …Can't see much.

MARSHALL   You're not using binoculars. You want to look through
           the binoculars?

           She takes one of his hands and clasps it.

           Ah, I see, well that's not a binocular, actually…

           He slips his hand out of hers.

           I… I'm kinda…

CLAIRE   Oh fuck this.

MARSHALL   I'm sorry, I'm just—

CLAIRE   Yeah.

MARSHALL   No listen—

CLAIRE   Yeah, yeah that's what I thought—

MARSHALL   But it's not, like, you, it's me, or it's girls, in general—

CLAIRE   Right, right, so you're gay—

MARSHALL   No, unfortunately not gay either, I just don't get it,
           I'm sorry, just not programmed that way, I don't even

understand how two people can even like each other enough to—

CLAIRE   Well fuck you too—

MARSHALL   You don't understand—

CLAIRE   Oh I understand perfectly, you think I'm too weird for you and I look ugly up close—

MARSHALL   No, I'm—

CLAIRE   Oh please, please! Don't make it worse! I got hit by a car for your sake, you cocksucker, and all you have to say to me is "I'm just not programmed that way?" You *asshole*—!

MARSHALL   For my sake—?

CLAIRE   Yeah, sure, why do you think I was standing in the middle of the road, huh!? I was coming to see you, I was coming to *make fucking contact,* and I looked up at your window apparently for just a second too long—

MARSHALL   I don't know if you can really blame me for that—

CLAIRE   Well I do! Murderer!

           She runs.

           BEN and LEON are alone in BEN's living room.

BEN   Get out of my house. You take your bag and you get out. Don't say anything. You get out.

LEON You don't understand—

BEN I don't need to.

LEON Yes you do need to, Ben, you need to cool down and hear me out, this is no way to treat a friend—

BEN Don't, no no no *don't*, please, would you please not use that word with me, would you *get* your fucking bag and go somewhere I can't see you—

LEON You really need to relax, Ben.

BEN Fuck you, get out.

LEON I don't appreciate that.

BEN Fuck you get out fuck you get out get the fuck out of my house, do you understand?

LEON This is very unlike you, Ben. If your wife and kid saw you—

BEN No, sorry, I don't think you understand the situation. You were a guest in my house, I didn't know you, I didn't *trust* you, *you were a guest in my house*. You took advantage. And now you are no longer welcome. Is that more clear?

LEON I never touched your wife without her permission.

BEN ...

LEON What, you gonna hit me? Hit me.

BEN ...

LEON   I look hard at you, Ben, and all I see is a sad little shit who's spent so much time hiding in the office he's afraid to fuck his wife.

BEN   Get out of my house.

LEON   With pleasure. Just as soon as we settle accounts.

BEN   Oh no no no, you son of a bitch, I don't owe you a—

LEON   Tell me, Ben, why do women flock to men like you, men without nerve? Your wife's far too good for you.

BEN   Maybe. But she's far too good for you too.

LEON   Oh yes, oh absolutely, your whole family is too good for me, your house, your little garden. Much too good for me. Cheque, please.

BEN   Do I have to forcibly remove you from my house?

LEON   Is that a rhetorical question?

BEN   Get out.

LEON   No no, I liked that other option, why don't you "forcibly remove me from your house," that sounded interesting.

BEN   Do I have to call the police?

LEON   What's that going to do, Ben? They'll make me go, but do you think I'll leave you alone, your family, your little garden? If that's what you think we really aren't as close as I thought—

BEN   You son of a bitch, if you so much as look at my family—

LEON   You'll get really angry, right? Your face will get all red just like now, right? Are you going to settle up with me or not?

        BEN spits in LEON's face.

        Ah. Ah yes. That's what I thought. And you know what, Ben? That's just fine. I've taken a security measure. You hear this?

        He shakes his duffle bag. Something rattles inside.

        Because I've got no legal way of collecting what I'm owed, I've resorted to taking some items of value from your bedroom. I've put a considerable amount of your wife's jewellery into my bag, along with a couple of your nicer watches and some cash that was on the dresser. I regret having to be so crude about it but that's the position you put me in with your unwillingness to share the wealth.

BEN   Are you joking?

LEON   Do you think I'm joking?

BEN   You're out of your mind. You know I won't let you leave the house with my stuff in your bag.

LEON   But that's the truly amazing thing. You will. You almost certainly will. Because what's going to happen, Ben? We'll grapple with the bag, we'll struggle, you'll pull and pull, but I'm a pretty strong guy and chances are I'll maintain my hold and you'll have to decide: what are you prepared to do? Are you gonna kill me? Are you gonna knock me unconscious? And I think in your honest, miserable heart of hearts the answer is no.

BEN   …

LEON   What are you prepared to do?

BEN   Have you not a shred of—?

LEON   What. Are you. Prepared. To do.

BEN   …

LEON   That's what I thought.

BEN   …

LEON   It was nice knowing you, Ben.

> *He leaves* BEN *standing in the doorway.* BEN's *arms hang limply at his side. He doesn't move.* LOLA *appears beside him.*
>
> *They're in their bedroom. She touches his chest. He won't look at her.*

BEN   You don't need to say anything.

> *She touches his face.*

           I… I trust you. I trust you. I'm not a jealous…

LOLA   Why won't you look at me?

BEN   I'm looking at you.

> *She moves her hand up his thigh. He pulls away from her.*

I'm sorry.

LOLA   Don't be sorry.

BEN   I'm sorry.

LOLA   Ben…

BEN   …

LOLA   Look at me, please? What are you thinking?

BEN   Did you find him… do you find that type of… did you find him romantic?

LOLA   …No. Not romantic.

BEN   Exciting? Did you find him exciting, did you think he was more alive somehow than I am or…?

LOLA   No, Ben, no, I didn't, I found him—

BEN   Interesting, you found him interesting.

LOLA   I love you, Ben, and that love is not contingent on whether your knuckles are rough or—

BEN   I'm not so different from him in many ways, you know, I could do all the same things, given different—

LOLA   Why are you afraid to touch me?

> *CLAIRE goes to her window. She looks out at MARSHALL's house, his windowsill (the window having been shattered); he's not there. Her face falls. She*

grabs her flashlight, turns it on and off a couple of times in quick succession to catch his attention should he be there to see it. Nothing happens. But then, snapping her flashlight on again, she notices something: a sign, pieces of paper taped together, is hung across the sill.

I'M SORRY, it says. PLEASE COME BACK.

LEON, across the street, is in shadow.

BEN   He's back.

BEN, CLAIRE and LOLA are in their house.

He's out there right now. Leon. He's parked across the street.

CLAIRE   Oh shit.

LOLA   Nice mouth, Claire. Why would he come back—?

BEN   I'm gonna do something.

LOLA   Just call the police, Ben.

BEN   No.

CLAIRE   Just call the police, Dad.

BEN   It's fine. It'll be fine.

LOLA   What are you going to do?

BEN   Let me take care of it.

LOLA	Ben—
BEN	This is an exceptional situation.
LOLA	I know that, but—
BEN	You know I don't believe that violence is a means to anything.

He rushes out.

LOLA	But why would he come back?

They're alone now, LOLA, CLAIRE and MARSHALL, alone together. There is a sense of ritual preparation, a sense of hush. MARSHALL comes to his window, watches.

CLAIRE	I see him right away.
LOLA	I see him too.
MARSHALL	I see him too.
CLAIRE	I watch my father go and I'm choking, I'm gasping, I can't catch my breath, and I'm afraid for Leon, I want to protect him, but why the fuck should I care about *him*?
LOLA	I want my husband to come home with blood on his hands.
MARSHALL	I lose sight of them so quickly.
CLAIRE	Because he's like me, because I'm like him, that must be it, because I'm broken like him, wrong like him— will somebody fix me, please?

LOLA	I want him to come home with blood on his hands and to take his hands and place them on my face.
MARSHALL	I lose sight of them so, so quickly.
CLAIRE	I'd give anything for someone to fix me and make me normal, you know, like a normal person, who wants normal things, and has a boyfriend, and has friend friends, and doesn't break people's windows, often, and falls in love at the age of fourteen and gets married and has lots of kids and a nicer, cleaner house than her mother's—you know: *normal*—is that possible? Can anybody make that possible for me, please?
LOLA	And tell me I exist.
CLAIRE	What a cruel, stupid joke! Why was I made able to love like fucking crazy but unable to earn love from anyone else?
LOLA	Not with words. With his hands on my face.
MARSHALL	I lose sight of them so, so quickly, and then I know nothing, because that's the limit, isn't it, what you can see of people, that's all you get to know, and that's dangerous, that kind of ignorance, too dangerous for me, thanks, from now on I'm keeping my binoculars trained on the sky, because you don't get hurt that way, because that way you don't find yourself waking up in the middle of the night unable to catch your breath, and you're fine, and you're okay, and you've got everything you need, by yourself, in your house, in your room, in your little darkened corner—from now on—from now on—
LOLA	And we'll bathe together and watch the blood wash off.

MARSHALL   I'll close my eyes. I'll watch the inside of my head. Why shouldn't that be enough?

CLAIRE   Can you give me a reason, one reason, one fucking little teensy tiny reason why I shouldn't find another speeding car and cross the street?

BEN   I follow him across the city. To his home. To the place where he sleeps.

             Sound of rapping at a door. Rapping harder, with more urgency, with more violence. Sound of a door opening. Light on BEN and LEON.

LEON   ...You.

             Black. Light rises on the faces of CLAIRE, LOLA and MARSHALL. Watching. Listening.

             Sounds of an apartment being torn to pieces: wood snapped, the legs kicked out from under a kitchen table; a toaster flung against tile; doors ripped off cupboards, food poured out of cans and boxes; pages and pages torn from books. And only a single human voice:

             Stop... please... please stop...

             But he's in darkness. Only the faces of CLAIRE, LOLA and MARSHALL. Watching. Listening.

             Sound of plates breaking, cutlery clattering onto tile. Sound of a knife slashing up a mattress, a pillow. Sound of a television smashed. And only a single human voice:

             No... no no no, Ben, no, no, no...

But darkness yet. Only the faces of CLAIRE, LOLA and MARSHALL. Watching. Listening.

Sound of glass breaking.

Crescendo.

Light on BEN and LEON in LEON's apartment.

BEN hits LEON in the face, breaking his nose. LEON falls. BEN kicks him. He kicks him again. LEON doesn't fight back. It goes on.

BEN stops.

Silence.

BEN stands above LEON, fixed to the spot. LEON is weeping. BEN is watching LEON weep. BEN's out of breath. Shaking.

God help me.

BEN   Tell me what I should do.

LEON   God help me. Somebody help me.

BEN   Tell me what I should do, tell me what's right, what would you do in my position?

BEN reaches out and takes LEON's hand. He squeezes LEON's hand, he wraps his fingers around LEON's fingers.

I barely know you. I barely even know you.

He takes LEON's hand into both of his.

I've got to go. I've got to go. I've got to get in my car and—

LEON   No.

BEN   …

LEON   No, would you just…

BEN   …

LEON   Just don't leave right this minute.

BEN   …

LEON   Could you just… stay here… a little longer…

BEN   …

LEON   And I'm not… I mean I don't want anything, nothing, I just… don't go.

BEN   …

LEON   Don't go.

BEN   I won't.

LEON   Don't go.

BEN   I'm not going.

LEON   Just five minutes.

BEN   ...

LEON   Okay. Okay.

BEN   It's okay. It's gonna be okay.

LEON   Just five minutes. Just stay here with me for five minutes.

BEN   ...

LEON   Okay. Okay.

BEN   ...

LEON   ...

> *Long silence.*

> *LOLA comes forward. She places her hands on BEN's shoulders.*

LOLA   Are we safe?

> *LOLA takes LEON's place. LEON is gone. The bedroom.*

BEN   I'd like you to tell me what you need from me.

LOLA   What do you mean?

BEN   What I said. Tell me what you need from me. I love you. I don't want to lose you.

LOLA   I never suggested—

> *He kisses her.*

...I need you to look at me. I need you to look at me and not look away.

BEN   And?

LOLA   No "and."

BEN   I can do that.

LOLA   And what do you need from me?

BEN   ...Tell me I'm a good man.

LOLA   ...

BEN   Or good enough.

> *She kisses him passionately. He kisses her back.*

MARSHALL   What can you see?

> *BEN and LOLA are gone.*

CLAIRE   Nothing. No lights on in the house.

MARSHALL   Does that mean we're alone?

> *They're in his bedroom. It's before dawn. CLAIRE looks through the binoculars. He looks at her. She lowers the binoculars. He moves ever so tentatively to touch her face.*

CLAIRE   ...I'm afraid of you.

MARSHALL   I don't think I'm going to hurt you.

CLAIRE   You don't think?

MARSHALL No. Not on purpose.

          A moment. He walks to the windowsill.

          Come here.

CLAIRE   …

MARSHALL I want you to see the sunrise break over the top of your
          chimney.

          She goes to him. They look.

CLAIRE   How long?

MARSHALL Moments.

          A beat. Another.

          The sun rises. Morning light finds their faces.

          So. Do you feel alive?

CLAIRE   …I don't know.

          He raises the binoculars to his eyes. Looks off, out.

          Marshall.

MARSHALL Yes?

CLAIRE   What are you looking at?

MARSHALL …

CLAIRE   Look at me.

> *A moment. Slowly, his binoculars pressed to his eyes, he turns to her.*

Can you see me?

> *He adjusts the focus on the binoculars. They're two feet apart.*

Am I there?

> *He takes a step closer to her.*

MARSHALL   My God.

CLAIRE   What is it?

MARSHALL   You're everywhere.

> *He steps closer to her. Almost touching her. The other end of the binoculars meets her face. The lenses press up against her eyes. His eyes and hers are connected. They stand like this together for a moment. Then, holding the binoculars in place, as one, they move their lips towards each other. Straining. They press and press. But their mouths won't reach. They are an unbridgeable inch apart.*

CLAIRE   It's difficult.

> *But they keep trying.*

Acknowledgements

I'm indebted first of all to the cast and crew of these two plays' premiere productions, all of whom gave generously of their time and talent. My gratitude to Brooke Banning, Tom Barnett, Monica Dottor, Jennifer Dowding, David Ferry, Anthony Furey, Brendan Gall, Joy Lachica, Natasha Mytnowych, Thomas Ryder Payne, Gary Reineke, Naomi Skwarna, Lyon Smith, André du Toit and the late, wonderful Gina Wilkinson.

Iris Turcott's passion and dramaturgical astuteness helped shepherd these plays into their finished forms, under the auspices of the Canadian Stage Company's Play Development Program.

Rena Zimmerman at Great North Artists Management offered insight, perspective and support.

The SummerWorks Theatre Festival, under the direction of Keira Loughran, provided a great launching pad for *In Full Light*.

The Tarragon Theatre's upstairs studio was a terrific home for *The Crossing Guard*. Richard Rose and Camilla Holland generously supported the production, Melanie Mooney gave us countless hours of assistance in sorting out the details and Verne Good's technical prowess made our show run smoothly.

Big Milly's Backyard in Kokrobite, Ghana, provided an oasis of stability that helped me write the first draft of *In Full Light*. I'm indebted to Ghana itself for the perspective to write that play and the emotional jolt that set it in motion.

The Absit Omen writing group contributed a helpful early reading of *In Full Light*.

Nicolas Billon, Anthony Furey, Melanie Leishman, Kevin Shea and Naomi Skwarna—wise and witty friends—read earlier versions of these plays and offered valuable feedback.

Philip Akin, Daniel Briere, Monica Dottor, Matthew Edison, Mark Ellis, Randy Hughson and Sarah Orenstein brought perceptiveness and talent to workshops of these plays at the Canadian Stage Company.

Brooke Banning, my brother Adam Karasik and my parents Roz and Lorne Karasik contributed measureless love and support.

Thanks, everybody.

Daniel Karasik was born in 1986. His award-winning plays have been seen in Toronto, New York and Germany. He has been a member of playwrights' units at Tarragon Theatre, Factory Theatre and the Canadian Stage Company, and was one of eight invited playwrights at the Stratford Shakespeare Festival's inaugural playwrights' retreat.

His play *The Innocents*—a hit at the SummerWorks Theatre Festival—was presented in New York by Bridge Theatre Company, and in German translation at the Staatstheater Mainz in Mainz, Germany, as part of their 2011/2012 season. In 2011 his play for children, *The Remarkable Flight of Marnie McPhee*, was produced by Carousel Players, touring schools across southern Ontario.

Daniel's poetry and fiction have appeared widely in literary magazines, and he is one of eleven new poets featured in *Undercurrents: New Voices in Canadian Poetry*, an anthology from Cormorant Books.

As an actor, Daniel has performed leading roles at Tarragon Theatre, the Arts Club Theatre and many others, as well as in film and television.

He lives in Toronto.

Printed on Silva Enviro 100% post-consumer EcoLogo certified paper, processed chlorine free and manufactured using biogas energy.